hric

APR 2010

How You Can Use

WASTE

ENERGY

to Heat and Light Your Home

Claire O'Neal

Mitchell Lane

P.O. Box 196
Hockessin, Delaware 19707
Visit us on the web: www.mitchelllane.com
Comments? email us: mitchelllane@mitchelllane.com

TRUCKS
THIS WAY

All About Electric and Hybrid Cars
Green Changes You Can Make Around Your Home
How to Harness Solar Power for Your Home
How to Use Wind Power to Light and Heat Your Home
How You Can Use Waste Energy to Heat
and Light Your Home

Copyright © 2010 by Mitchell Lane Publishers

All rights reserved. No part of this book may be reproduced without written permission from the publisher. Printed and bound in the United States of America.

Special thanks to Jimmy of the City of Newark Public Works Department –C.O.

Printing 1 2 3 4 5 6 7 8 9

Library of Congress Cataloging-in-Publication Data

O'Neal, Claire.
  How to use waste energy to heat and light your home / by Claire O'Neal.
    p. cm. — (Tell your parents)
  Includes bibliographical references and index.
  ISBN 978-1-58415-765-6 (library bound)
  1. Cogeneration of electric power and heat—Juvenile literature. 2. Recycling (Waste, etc.)—Juvenile literature. 3. Waste products as fuel—Juvenile literature. I. Title.
  TK1041.O67 2009
  621.1'99—dc22

                                2009004483

                                PLB

CONTENTS

Words in **bold** type can be found in the glossary.

Landfill

TRASH INTO TREASURE

Late in the afternoon, Jimmy pulls his truck to the curb of 42 Apple Road, the last house on his route in Newark, Delaware. He's visited around 800 houses today. He waves at the two kids watching him from the window. As he pushes a button on his huge dashboard, an automated arm reaches out from his truck to the dark green plastic can on the curb. A large claw on the arm grips the can tightly, picking it up and turning it upside down over a hole in the side of the truck. Jimmy can't see from where he's sitting, but the kids watch as their trash falls into the hole—three large tied white plastic bags from the kitchen trash can, plastic cups and juice boxes from recent trips to McDonald's, and the old car seat they don't need anymore.

Garbage truck

An opossum looks for dinner in a trash can

Jimmy's waste collection vehicle—known to most as a garbage truck—is topped out now. His truck has crusher blades inside that smash the garbage to make room for more, but 10 tons of trash is as much as it can handle. It's time to make the 23-mile trip to the Pine Tree Corners transfer station. There, Jimmy backs up a ramp to a barn-like building. He revs the engine and flips levers and switches that tip the loader back. A pusher blade inside the truck squeezes a long, compressed log of trash out of the loader and onto the concrete floor. Jimmy pays the transfer station attendant $615 for the load, and he is on his way back to the Newark city yards, where he'll park his truck until tomorrow.

The trash, of course, has a different destination. A backhoe pushes Jimmy's compressed load across the floor of the transfer station and into a waiting trailer, already packed with other loads of the day. When full, a semi-truck will take the trailer to one of three landfills in Delaware. The nearest one is Cherry Island Landfill in Wilmington. There, the trailer's load is carried up to the open part of the landfill, called the **active face**, by enormous dump trucks. Jimmy's load finds its final resting place along with many others in a pile that grows by nearly 2,000 tons daily.

The kids at 42 Apple Road probably don't think much about their trash. Twice a week, Jimmy makes it disappear. But the scope of our growing trash problem is overwhelming.

A landfill compactor presses trash into the landfill. These tractors, which weigh up to 50 tons, have specialized blades and wheels to smash down the mixed materials in trash.

Front-end loaders inside a waste transfer station move trash into waiting trailers. Waste companies save money and gas by unloading trash at centrally located waste transfer stations instead of faraway landfills.

The average American throws away 4.5 pounds of stuff each day, from banana peels and milk jugs to old homework sheets and broken toys. A classroom of 20 kids makes 90 pounds of trash every day! Most of this trash—over 55 percent—goes into landfills.

Few people realize that inside each landfill lies a reservoir of untapped energy. Instead of going to the landfill, trash could be taken to a **waste-to-energy** (WTE) power plant. These plants burn trash in a controlled way to release the energy in our garbage. In 2009, the WTE plants in the United States were delivering heat to buildings and making enough

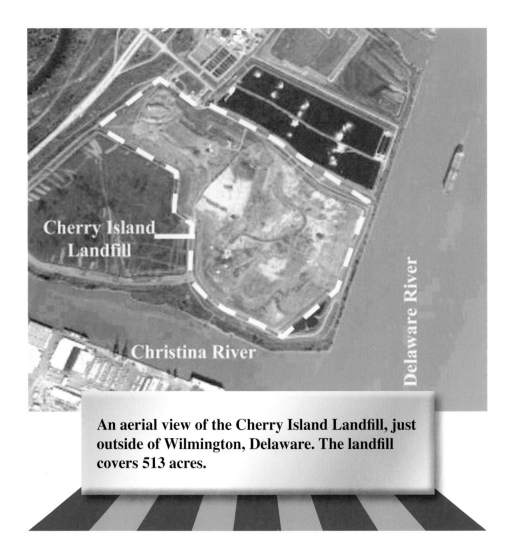

Cherry Island Landfill

Christina River

Delaware River

An aerial view of the Cherry Island Landfill, just outside of Wilmington, Delaware. The landfill covers 513 acres.

electricity to power nearly 3 million homes. We will always make garbage, so why not turn our trash into energy treasure?

WTE is especially attractive now because it addresses our trash crisis and our energy crisis at the same time. Recent spikes in energy prices, including gasoline and heating bills, interest many consumers in **alternative energy** sources. Like wind and solar power, WTE doesn't rely on traditional sources

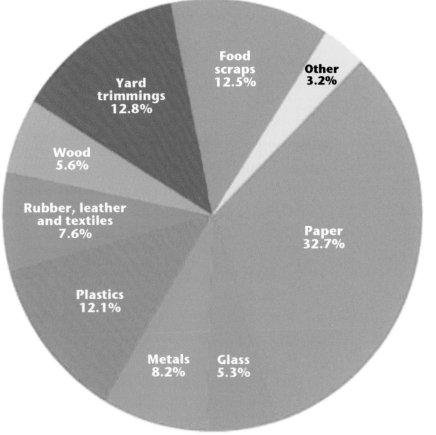

Total Municipal Solid Waste Generation (by material), 2007
254 Million Tons (before recycling)

- Food scraps 12.5%
- Other 3.2%
- Yard trimmings 12.8%
- Wood 5.6%
- Rubber, leather and textiles 7.6%
- Plastics 12.1%
- Metals 8.2%
- Glass 5.3%
- Paper 32.7%

What makes up American garbage? It may surprise you. This pie chart shows that much of our waste—paper, plastics, metals, glass, and rubber—could be recycled.

like nuclear energy or **fossil fuels**—which include petroleum, natural gas, and coal. Traditional energy sources are cheap and abundant, but they have serious drawbacks.

A full kitchen-sized trash bag has enough stored energy to light a 100-watt lightbulb for 24 hours.

For one, our supply of fossil fuels will not last forever. It took millions of years in the earth for the remains of plants and animals to change into fossil fuels. We use these limited resources faster than they can be replaced. We don't know for certain how much fossil fuel remains underground, but geologists can make predictions. The U.S. Geological Survey forecasts that world oil supplies will begin to run out as early as 2075. Scientist Gregson Vaux predicts that we may have only 100 more years of coal left.

Using traditional energy sources has serious consequences for the environment as well. Nuclear power plants get their energy from rods of enriched uranium, which is radioactive and deadly. Each year, a large nuclear power facility needs to replace about 3 cubic yards of uranium, which will continue to be radioactive for another 1,000 years. The spent fuel sits in holding tanks at the power plants while governments around the world argue about how best to dispose of it.

Meanwhile, much scientific evidence blames fossil fuels for global warming. During the past two centuries, the burning of fossil fuels has pumped abnormal amounts of **carbon dioxide** gas into the atmosphere. This gas traps the sun's heat in the atmosphere, the same way glass traps heat in a greenhouse. The ten hottest years on record have occurred since 1990. The National Oceanic and Atmospheric Administration (NOAA)

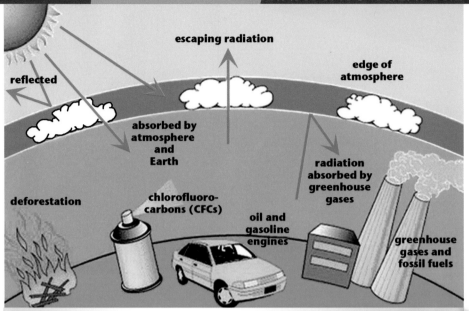

escaping radiation

edge of atmosphere

reflected

absorbed by atmosphere and Earth

radiation absorbed by greenhouse gases

deforestation

chlorofluoro-carbons (CFCs)

oil and gasoline engines

greenhouse gases and fossil fuels

Greenhouse gases heat up the earth by trapping the sun's energy. These gases are naturally occurring, like carbon dioxide, or human-made, like chlorofluorocarbons (CFCs). Burning coal in a power plant or gasoline in a car creates extra carbon dioxide that may be causing global warming. Trees could take up the extra carbon dioxide, but their help is limited because of worldwide deforestation. Waste energy technologies can reduce carbon dioxide levels, because burning trash releases less carbon dioxide than burning fossil fuels.

reports that if the warming trend continues, heat waves will increase. Sea levels will rise as glaciers and polar ice caps melt, affecting coastal cities around the globe.

Clearly, we are in the middle of both a trash crisis and an energy crisis. Both affect our daily lives, our future, and our planet. But you can make a difference, starting today, with the choices you make. Everyone benefits when we make less waste and use less electricity. Read on to learn how you can help, and how the waste we do make can be used in resourceful ways to help us overcome our energy problems.

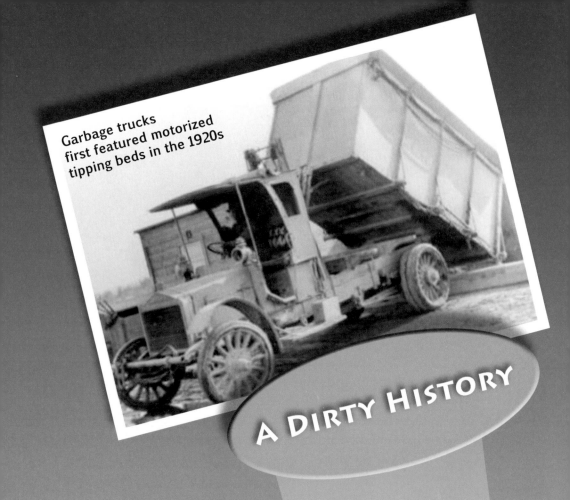

Garbage trucks first featured motorized tipping beds in the 1920s

A DIRTY HISTORY

Trash first became a problem when people began living together in large cities. One household off by itself may have burned its trash or dumped it in a hole, swamp, or river nearby. With thousands of households living in one town or city, trash disposal required a plan. The first city dump on record opened in 500 BCE, when the Greek city of Athens decreed that all garbage must be dumped at least one mile outside the city walls.

In Europe during the Middle Ages, conditions were not as sanitary. In 1400, Paris struggled to defend itself from invaders because it was hard to see around the massive wall of garbage that surrounded the town. In other cities, residents threw their trash—including toilet contents—into the street or in rivers flowing through the town. Mice, cockroaches, and

Thomas Edison

Scientists examine Black Death rats

germs thrived in the filth. In the 1340s, flea-ridden rats transmitted the Black Death, a disease that killed one-quarter to one-half of the entire population of Europe. Drinking water contaminated by waste led to fatal diarrhea caused by cholera and typhoid fever, which killed off whole villages. For the sake of public health, governments stepped in to take the trash away. Starting in the 1400s, European sanitation workers scoured the streets with horse-drawn carts, raking up waste by hand and taking it to trash piles outside cities.

New York City created America's first big trash problem in the mid-1800s. City horses posed the biggest health threat. Every day, Manhattan's horses left half a million pounds of manure and 45,000 gallons of urine behind as they walked through the streets. Dead horses also littered the city. Too

The Rubbish Carter, an engraving by Henry Mayhew. Rubbish carters from nineteenth-century London picked up dry trash, or rubbish, on the streets and took it to the city dump. There, poor women and children picked through the rubbish and saved anything that could be sold.

big to move, the carcasses were often left in the streets—to be eaten by dogs and bacteria—until they were a more manageable weight. Then they would be dumped in rivers or burned to make fertilizer or glue. In 1880 alone, 15,000 horse carcasses were removed from the streets of Manhattan.

In 1874, British engineers in Nottingham, England, came up with a novel solution to everyone's trash problem. They used heat from an **incinerator**—a stove that burns trash—to power an electricity generator. The generator wasn't new. British scientist Michael Faraday built the first electricity generator, called a dynamo, over 50 years earlier. But previous generators relied on wood or coal. Using trash greatly reduced the space needed for trash piles. When Thomas Edison developed the electric lightbulb in 1879, society quickly became dependent on electricity. During the next thirty years, over 250 of these first WTE power plants, called destructors, sprang up all over Britain. It wasn't long, however, before residents complained of fumes, ash, and bits of burning paper falling around their homes. Destructors fell into disuse by 1945.

America's first incinerator was built in 1885 on Governor's Island in New York, though people preferred the convenience of the open trash piles around New York City. In 1895, the city instituted regular garbage pickups. Street cleaners and garbage men took away waste before it could become infested with germs, greatly improving the survival rates of babies and children. But by the late 1930s, city dumps were crawling with mice and cockroaches. Angry citizens urged the city to use its 22 garbage incinerators instead. Their smoke wrapped the island of Manhattan in a permanent cloud.

Relief came in 1937, when Jean Vincenz, the Commissioner of Public Works in Fresno, California, invented modern landfills.

In some cities, garbage pick-up services are handled by street cleaners, who use their brooms and baskets to remove garbage from city streets.

Instead of an open dump, Vincenz's "sanitary landfill" was covered each day by a thin layer of dirt. The covering kept out rats and kept in odors. The idea caught on quickly with the military during World War II. By the 1950s, everyone's trash went to a sanitary landfill, and just in time. Thanks to the war, the U.S. experienced an economic boom in the 1950s. With more money in their pockets, Americans bought new clothes, appliances, and cars. They indulged in conveniences like disposable plates and diapers, paper towels, and napkins. America's increased wastefulness was helped by new garbage trucks, which featured enclosed trash compartments and hydraulic rams to cram more into one load. Landfills were built in less populated areas so that people never had to think about their trash once it left the

DID YOU KNOW...

The largest landfill in the world is Fresh Kills landfill on Staten Island, the southernmost part of New York City. Fresh Kills was opened as a temporary landfill in 1948, but it remained open until 2001. It is 225 feet high, taller than the Statue of Liberty, and covers 2,200 acres.

curb. No one recycled. Why would they when space and resources seemed limitless?

While the new landfills looked and smelled better from the top, they became underground reservoirs of poison. Liquid from the trash, called **leachate**, seeped into the soil at the bottom of landfills. Leachate contaminated dirt all around the landfill with heavy metals and toxic compounds. The toxins often made their way into groundwater, poisoning the public's drinking supply as well. The decomposing trash also created polluting and explosive gases that escaped into the atmosphere.

In the 1980s and 1990s, the U.S. Environmental Protection Agency (EPA) cracked down on landfills. The EPA mandated that all landfills must have a thick, protective bottom liner,

Diagram of a Modern Landfill

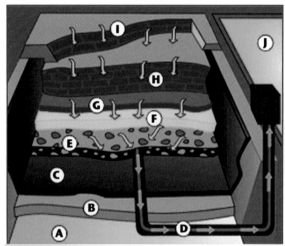

A. Ground Water
B. Clay
C. Plastic Liner
D. Leachate Collection Pipe
E. Gravel
F. Drainage Layer
G. Soil Layer
H. Old Garbage Cells
I. New Garbage Cells
J. Leachate Pond

Unlike the polluting city dumps of long ago, modern landfills are state-of-the-art waste containment systems. Layers of clay, plastic, and gravel line the bottom to protect the soil. Pipes collect leachate as the liquid filters down, carrying it away from the landfill to be treated and disposed of safely.

as well as collection systems for gases and leachate. The new rules made modern landfills safer, but the updates were expensive. Those that couldn't afford them closed down without cleaning up. Many old dumps and landfills are **Superfund sites** today. They are so hazardous to people and the environment that the government must step in and take special measures to clean the soil and water so that people living and working nearby don't get sick.

Today's landfills are much cleaner, but we fill them up faster than ever. The European Union has made member nations agree to cut back on landfill deposits by a staggering 65 percent, stating that there simply isn't the space for more landfills. What can't be recycled must be burned, much of it

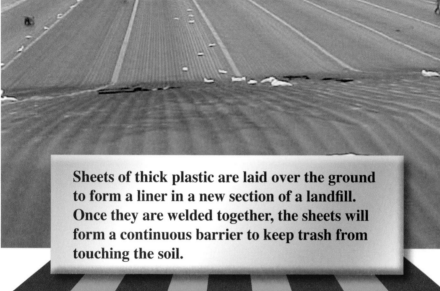

Sheets of thick plastic are laid over the ground to form a liner in a new section of a landfill. Once they are welded together, the sheets will form a continuous barrier to keep trash from touching the soil.

for energy. Europe has most of the 600 WTE plants around the globe, with Denmark, Sweden, and the Netherlands leading the way. Antonio Bonomo, of the Italian WTE company ASM, said, "In the U.S., there has been no commitment to energy saving. But now that the price of energy is much higher, and it will go even higher, then from this perspective, there is a good opportunity for investment."

In the past, WTE has met with strong opposition from communities that remembered polluting incinerators. Unlike Europe, the U.S. still has land available for landfills. But most communities don't want them, either. "Landfills have a modern life of fifteen to twenty years. Just think of that," says Nikolas Themelis, an engineer at Columbia University. With modern incinerators at their cleanest yet, Themelis and others think the time is right for Americans to give WTE another look.

Waste-to-Energy Plant in Coventry, UK

ENERGY FROM TRASH

In 2009, ninety waste-to-energy plants were in operation in the United States. The way in which WTE plants generate electricity is nearly identical to traditional, fossil-fuel-based plants. The only difference is the fuel. First, the waste is brought to a loading dock, where workers pick out large metal pieces and material that would be dangerous to burn. In some plants, the waste also travels past magnets that pick out smaller pieces. Metals like aluminum and steel do not burn well but can easily be recycled. Covanta Energy, which owns over thirty WTE plants in the United States alone, recycles enough metal each year to build 275,000 hybrid cars.

Next the waste is burned in a boiler, eight tons at a time, where the fire is stoked to 2,000 degrees Fahrenheit. At

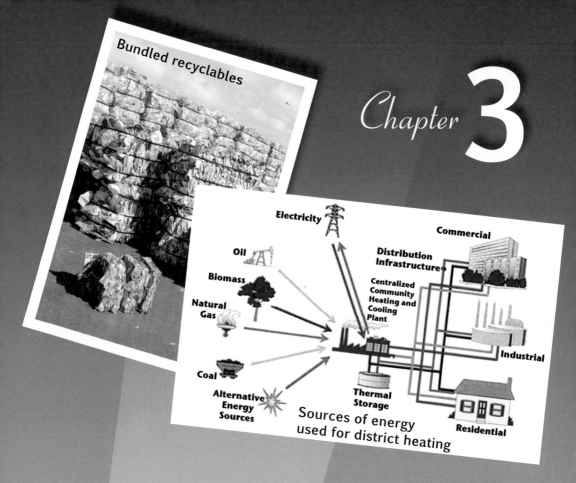

Bundled recyclables

Sources of energy used for district heating

temperatures this high, almost everything in the trash is neutralized and disintegrates into ash. Water-filled pipes line the boiler; the heat turns the water into steam. The steam from the pipes pushes blades on turbines to generate electricity, which flows into the **power grid** for customers to use. The incinerator at the American Ref-Fuel WTE plant in Newark, New Jersey, uses two turbines to generate 67 megawatts of power each hour, enough to power 50,000 homes near New York City.

Continuing WTE's spirit of resourcefulness, many plants go a step further. The boiler generates an enormous amount of heat. Instead of wasting the heat, steam from the pipes surrounding the boiler at the Baltimore, Maryland, RESCO plant is piped all the way to the city's downtown. There, the

Workers at a WTE plant pick through trash, taking out objects that are dangerous to burn. They wear thick rubber gloves and respirators to protect themselves from the garbage.

steam is used to heat buildings in the winter, and water vapor in the pipes cools them in the summer. This method is called **district heating**. Because heating and cooling needs account for the most energy use, district heating saves an enormous amount of electricity, far more than the WTE plant could make.

Back in the WTE plant, the fiery trash in the incinerator generates hot gas that contains toxins from the plastics, household chemicals, and batteries that may be burned together. The gas must be purified before it can be released to the atmosphere. First, it passes through filters called

scrubbers that use simple chemicals, like carbon, ammonia, and lime, to neutralize most impurities. Next, the air passes through special filters that pull floating particles out of the gas. After burning is complete, particles trapped by the smokestack fall to the ash pile at the bottom of the incinerator. Finally, the purified gas is tested and released from the plant's smokestack.

Incinerating the trash this way not only produces energy, but also reduces the volume of each 8-ton load of trash to

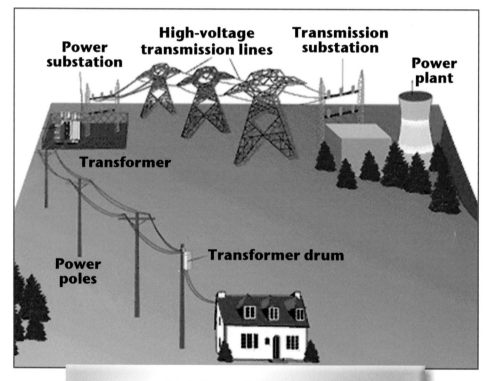

High-voltage transmission lines

Power substation

Transmission substation

Power plant

Transformer

Transformer drum

Power poles

The power grid delivers electricity from the power plant to homes and businesses. Modern grids use alternating current (AC) electricity, which can travel long distances without losing power.

The Spittelau district heating plant and incinerator in Vienna, Austria, opened in 1971. In 2008, it provided heat to 60,000 homes.

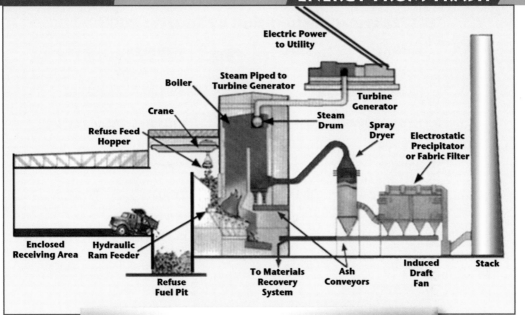

Electric Power to Utility

Boiler

Steam Piped to Turbine Generator

Crane

Turbine Generator

Steam Drum

Refuse Feed Hopper

Spray Dryer

Electrostatic Precipitator or Fabric Filter

Enclosed Receiving Area **Hydraulic Ram Feeder**

Refuse Fuel Pit

To Materials Recovery System

Ash Conveyors

Induced Draft Fan

Stack

A waste-to-energy plant. Burning trash generates heat and electricity (top), but also smoke that must be treated and filtered before it leaves the facility (bottom).

1 to 2 tons of ash. This makes a huge impact on how fast we fill landfills. The ash can contain concentrated levels of poisonous heavy metals like cadmium and lead, so it must be tested before disposal. If it is safe, the ash is compressed into pellets for easy storage and transportation. Most of the ash will go to a landfill, but about one-third of the safe ash will be reused to make landfill cover, cement block, or roads.

WTE is considered **renewable** energy because we will always make trash. Garbage is not as efficient of a fuel as fossil fuels, however. It takes 2,000 pounds of garbage to produce the same amount of electricity as a barrel of oil, or

U.S. Energy Consumption by Source, 2007

 BIOMASS 3.6%
renewable
Heating, electricity, transportation

 PETROLEUM 37.5%
nonrenewable
Transporation, manufacturing

 HYDROPOWER 2.4%
renewable
Electricity

 NATURAL GAS 23.3%
nonrenewable
Heating, manufacturing, electricity

 GEOTHERMAL 0.3%
renewable
Heating, electricity

 COAL 22.5%
nonrenewable
Electricity, manufacturing

 WIND 0.3%
renewable
Electricity

 URANIUM 8.3%
nonrenewable
Electricity

 SOLAR 0.1%
renewable
Light, heating, electricity

 PROPANE 1.7%
nonrenewable
Manufacturing, heating

Source: Energy Information Administration, Annual Energy Review, 2007

Most of U.S. energy—93.3%—comes from petroleum, natural gas, and coal. Only 6.7% of U.S. energy currently comes from renewable sources. The largest renewable source today is biomass, a category that includes WTE.

500 pounds of coal. But with New York City alone producing 12,000 tons of garbage a day, we are not likely to run out of trash anytime soon.

Because it is so much like a traditional power plant, WTE is relatively easy to start using, compared to other alternative energies. Solar and wind power require special, expensive equipment as well as an appropriate location (one with lots of sun or wind). However, unlike solar and wind power, WTE

DID YOU KNOW...

Wheelabrator Technologies opened the first large-scale WTE plant in the U.S. in 1975 near Boston, Massachusetts. By 2009, the facility was burning over 1,500 tons of waste each day, providing power to 47,000 homes.

is not a completely clean energy. Smoke from trash incinerators contains toxins, including heavy metals, chlorine, and hydrochloric acid (a component of acid rain). Improved technology removes up to 99.7 percent of these toxins from the air as it leaves the factory. However, WTE opponents argue that the poisons are concentrated in the ash instead of the air, which ends up in landfills and could leach out and pollute the soil or groundwater. WTE advocates argue that ash is actually safer than regular trash, because the incinerator's high temperatures break down many of the dangerous compounds in garbage.

Regardless of what is burned, however, WTE is cleaner than fossil-fuel-based energy. In fact, the EPA considers WTE one of the cleanest forms of energy available. Overall, energy from trash has a smaller **carbon footprint**—the amount of carbon dioxide put in the atmosphere—than fossil fuels. Consider the pollution caused by equipment and trucks used in fossil fuel mining operations, as well as the additional trucks or rail cars that take the coal or oil to the power plant. Using trash instead helps reduce those costs to our environment.

WHY TRASH OUR PLANET?

Landfill Gas and Biogas Dryer

CREATIVE USES FOR LANDFILL GAS

Policy experts agree that WTE makes the best of a trashy situation, but it isn't the only answer to either our trash or our energy needs. In 2009, only 17 percent of American trash was being burned for energy. Even Denmark, the world leader in WTE, burns only 54 percent of its trash. We will still need landfills for the ash and for items that cannot be burned. Luckily, the landfill itself can contribute to our quest for cleaner energy—through landfill gas.

Decomposing trash in landfills creates landfill gas, which bubbles up through layers of trash and is released into the air. The gas is made of mostly carbon dioxide and **methane**. Methane is the most powerful greenhouse gas, trapping 21 times more heat than carbon dioxide. Methane is also the major component of **natural gas**, a commonly used household

Landfill Gas Data Tester

Pipeline delivering landfill gas

fuel. Just like natural gas, methane can explode. Because of these dangers, the EPA requires that modern landfills destroy landfill gas before it leaves the site. Pipes inserted into the landfill capture the gas and direct it to a flame, where it burns in a controlled way.

More than 420 U.S. landfills are now putting this gas to a better use, often in creative ways. The Southeastern Chester County landfill (SECCRA) in suburban Philadelphia pipes its landfill gas to an electricity generator built right on top of the landfill. There, the methane in the landfill gas is burned to power a turbine, just like a mini power plant. SECCRA Power came online in 2007, and within two years was supplying electricity to 500 homes. It followed the lead of other organizations like the East Kentucky Power Cooperative

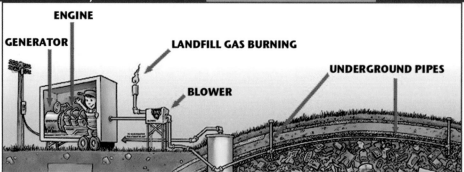

ENGINE
GENERATOR
LANDFILL GAS BURNING
UNDERGROUND PIPES
BLOWER

Landfill gas is collected in pipes driven into the landfill. In most landfills, these pipes deliver the gas to a flame, where it is destroyed. Today, a growing number of landfills route the gas instead to an engine that powers an electricity generator.

(EKPC). In 2003, EKPC began harvesting methane from three different landfills to power generators. Their program provides 8.8 megawatts of energy, powering up to 8,000 homes.

Landfill gas doesn't have to stay at the landfill, however. Organizations and companies are beginning to explore the possibilities of dependable, cleaner energy from landfill gas. Other alternative energies require special equipment that is often expensive, such as a wind turbine for wind power, and solar panels for solar power. But landfill gas doesn't require a lot of system changes. After a few modifications to boilers or furnaces, landfill gas can be used in much the same way as natural gas.

Pattonville High School in Maryland Heights, Missouri, provides a small-scale example. The school's next-door neighbor is the Fred Weber landfill. A pioneer in district heating, the construction-oriented landfill already used its own gas to heat its asphalt and concrete mixing plants. When the school's ecology club came up with the idea to use landfill gas to heat their school, Fred Weber built a 3,600-foot pipeline to bring landfill gas to the high school's basement furnace. Because Fred Weber donates the gas, the school saves $27,000 every year in heating costs.

One of the biggest landfill gas success stories comes from the BMW manufacturing plant in Spartanburg, South Carolina. The upscale car company built a 9.5-mile-long pipeline to transport filtered and **dehydrated** landfill gas all the way from the guts of the Palmetto Landfill to the energy center of the BMW plant. At the energy center, boilers burn landfill-generated methane to power a four-turbine, 4.4-megawatt energy station. The station supplies 25 percent of

These landfill gas–powered generators supply the U.S. Coast Guard Yard in Baltimore, Maryland, with electricity and heat. The base, which repairs all the Coast Guard's ships, is the first Coast Guard facility entirely powered by renewable energy.

A diagram of a bioreactor landfill. Pipes transport leachate from the bottom of the landfill to a treatment station. The leachate is treated —either with air, chemicals, or helpful bacteria—and then injected into the top layers of the landfill. As the treated leachate trickles down through the landfill's layers, it encourages faster breakdown of trash. Faster breakdown produces more landfill gas. Different pipes collect the gas and, in some cases, deliver it to an electricity generator.

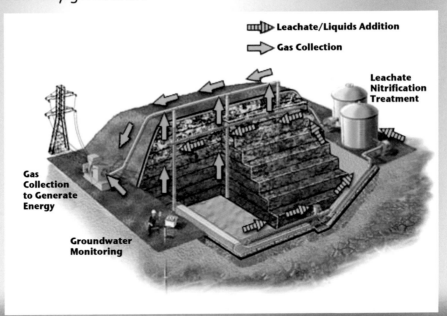

the factory's electricity needs. It also meets nearly all of the plant's heating and cooling needs, thanks to the pipes from the boilers that run through buildings all over the property. In total, nearly 70 percent of the plant's energy now comes from landfill gas and not from the power grid.

BMW's engineers were so pleased with the results that they turned their green eyes to the paint shop, the biggest

A Landfill Gas Compressor

energy user in the plant. In the paint shop, car parts are painted and then baked dry in 23 ovens, which were originally powered by natural gas. Now, landfill gas directly supplies all the power to the ovens. The heat from the ovens is also used to heat the facility during colder months.

Since 2003, BMW's many creative efforts have saved the company over $8 million in energy costs. Their contract with the landfill protects them from price increases that worry most customers of grid-based electricity. Because they have cut their power use from the grid by more than two-thirds, they also estimate that they have prevented over 216,000 tons of carbon dioxide from entering the atmosphere. BMW is the first car company in the world with a painting operation powered by green energy.

Burning methane releases carbon dioxide into the atmosphere, as does burning natural gas. But landfill gas provides energy that would otherwise come from conventional fossil fuel sources that create even more carbon dioxide and other, nastier pollutants. Also, landfill gas tends to be used near its source, unlike electricity from traditional power plants. And unlike fossil fuels, many energy scientists consider landfill methane a renewable resource because we will continue to need landfills. The future of trash looks a little brighter if those landfills can provide energy, too.

It's important to keep in mind that WTE is not an ideal solution to the trash or energy crises. That we can harvest any energy at all from our waste is a great perk, but the real value of WTE is that it reduces the amount of waste we put in a landfill. Waste management experts see a future in which WTE works alongside individual efforts to recycle and reuse waste, all with the goal of keeping landfills as small as possible.

Take a look at what you throw away. Could you reuse it instead? For example, do you have an old computer, television set, or sweater that you don't use anymore? If it's in good shape, you could donate it to a charity, like Goodwill or the Salvation Army. Some charities even drive to your doorstep to pick up your old stuff. Do you have old books and

Carting recyclables

Chapter 5

Recycling bins

Paper

Plastic

Glass

magazines? Hospitals and nursing homes may appreciate them. And instead of throwing out a torn-up T-shirt, maybe you could cut it into squares and use them as rags. The shirt stays out of the landfill, and by using rags, you'll send fewer paper towels there, too.

Next time, think twice before you throw your stuff out. Our culture makes us feel as if we need things that we don't, especially when something new or convenient is invented. Commercials encourage us to buy the latest toys, cell phones, and computers when old ones might work just fine. We talk about throwing trash "away," but it will never disappear from the earth. We will always make trash, but making less of it is one of the easiest and biggest ways you can help the environment.

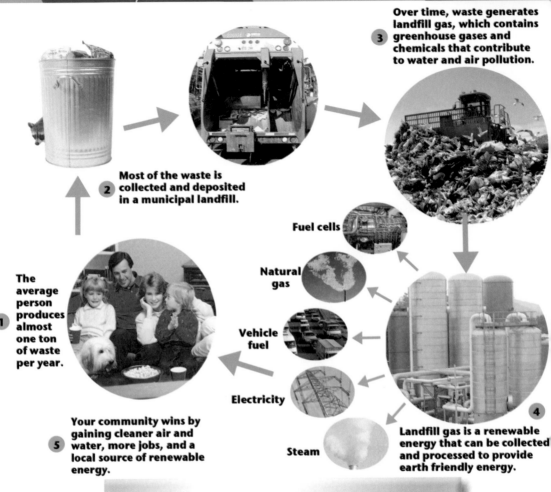

3 Over time, waste generates landfill gas, which contains greenhouse gases and chemicals that contribute to water and air pollution.

2 Most of the waste is collected and deposited in a municipal landfill.

Fuel cells

Natural gas

1 The average person produces almost one ton of waste per year.

Vehicle fuel

Electricity

Steam

5 Your community wins by gaining cleaner air and water, more jobs, and a local source of renewable energy.

4 Landfill gas is a renewable energy that can be collected and processed to provide earth friendly energy.

Burning waste for energy does not eliminate the need for landfills. Burning landfill gas for energy turns a nasty pollutant and greenhouse gas into a cleaner, renewable energy source.

"Garbologist" William Rathje knows that you can learn a lot about people by looking at their trash. Rathje and his anthropology students at the University of Arizona founded the Garbage Project after the first Earth Day in 1970. What they found surprised everyone. Landfills aren't full of disposable diapers or Styrofoam cups. In fact, those together account for less than 2 percent of landfill volume. The biggest chunk, making up nearly half of what the project dug up, was paper that could have been recycled.

Recycling paper, plastics, metal, and glass is a great way to start cleaning up the environment. Right now, Americans recycle 31 percent of their waste, but the number could easily be higher. Recycling centers sell the materials they collect to processing facilities, where they are made into new products. Used aluminum cans are melted down and made into new ones. Unbroken, used glass bottles are simply washed and filled again. Used plastic soda bottles or milk jugs are shredded, melted, and re-formed into new plastic bottles, toys, or even fibers to make fleece jackets. Not only does recycling keep our landfill smaller, it also conserves raw materials and energy. For example, because aluminum cans are thin and pure, it takes 95 percent less energy to melt them and re-form them into a new can than to do the same with raw aluminum ore mined from the earth.

Unfortunately, many producers don't use recycled materials. It's usually cheaper for them to buy new ones. For example, because wood prices are low, paper manufacturers cut down thousands of acres of forests a year just to make toilet paper. The environmental group Greenpeace states that Americans could save 400,000 trees if each family bought just one roll of 100 percent recycled toilet paper.

The power to change what goes into our landfills is in your hands. Take a closer look at what you and your parents buy. Choose paper and plastic products made from **post-consumer content**, which means they are made of material put in recycling bins by people just like you.

Another great and disgustingly fun way to keep your trash can emptier is to reuse potato peels, moldy grapes, or autumn leaves. Nearly 13 percent of municipal waste comes

HOME RECYCLABLES

paper bags and shredded paper

newspapers

phone books

magazines and brochures

junk mail and envelopes

paper

cardboard

miscellaneous boxes

plastic bags

glass

plastics

tin and aluminum cans

RECYCLING BINS

If your local trash authority doesn't offer curbside pickup, you can take your recyclables to a recycling bin or drop them off at a recycling facility.

OTHER RECYCLABLES

Please check with your local waste authority about what other things you can recycle. Some facilities can dispose of electronics; hazardous household waste; motor oil; oil filters; tires; old clothing, shoes, and other materials that can't be donated; lightbulbs; wood; and so on.

Encourage your family and friends to recycle. Working together, we can make a big difference!

A compost pile helps yard waste and kitchen scraps decompose, turning them into a nutritious food for plants around your yard. Compost piles are easy to build and maintain.

from food, and another 13 percent from your yard, including mown grass. Instead of throwing this plant waste away, why not compost it? Your town may have a community compost pile, where your personal green waste goes into making mulch for parks and public spaces. If not, you can build your own compost pile, or buy a compost bin from a home improvement or garden store. After a few months in a compost bin, your kitchen scraps will become rich, dark food for the garden, and they will stay out of the landfill.

Finally, be curious about what happens to the trash you make. Do you know where your waste goes? If you don't know, you can find out. In some areas, your family may be able to choose who collects your trash. If so, you can pick the carrier that takes your trash to the greenest landfill or to a WTE plant. In the meantime, you can do your part to keep trash out of the landfill by reusing and recycling what you can, and by making smart choices about what you buy.

Try This!

Start a Garden with Empty Toilet Paper Rolls

Ever thought about starting a vegetable garden? Growing your own food is not only great for your health, but also for the environment. The food your mom or dad buys from the grocery store has usually been transported across the country. It requires boxes, wraps, and packaging, much of which will end up in a landfill. The trucks that deliver the food to the grocery store also deliver tons of carbon dioxide into the air. Growing your own food takes a little extra time and effort, but it's a win-win for your body and for the earth!

Vegetables are a great choice for beginners. They are easy to grow. And many kinds—such as tomatoes, peppers, green beans, herbs, and more—grow well in pots, indoors or out. Get started today by reusing empty toilet paper or paper towel rolls to make your own seed pots. Almost any kind of veggie will work with this method. You can even start a fruit tree this way!

You will need:
empty toilet paper or paper towel rolls
scissors
tray or cookie sheet with rim
potting soil
seeds
large pot or garden

1. Cut toilet paper rolls in half, and paper towel rolls in half again. This makes two seed pots per toilet paper roll and four per paper towel roll.
2. To form a flat bottom for each pot, carefully fold the paper around the end of each roll toward the middle. Set each new pot, bottom-down, on a tray or cookie sheet.
3. Fill the paper rolls with potting soil and plant two or three seeds in each roll.
4. Set the tray of rolls in a warm, sunny spot. Water every day or so and watch your seeds sprout!

5. After a few weeks, your seedlings will be big enough to transplant to a pot or garden. Hold each roll under its bottom when you pick it up so that the soil won't fall out. Dig a hole the size of the roll where you want the seedling to go, then set the roll in the dirt and cover it over. You don't need to remove the roll—the seedling's roots will break up the paper for you as they grow.

6. Take care of your new plants and enjoy the fruits (or vegetables) of your labor!

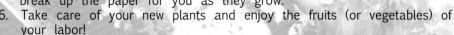

Historical Timeline

500 BCE The first city dump on record is sited outside the walls of Athens, Greece.

1340s The Black Death wipes out half the population of Europe.

1690 America's first paper mill opens in Philadelphia. The Rittenhouse Paper Mill makes paper from used paper and recycled cotton and linen.

1821 Michael Faraday invents the dynamo to induce electricity.

1874 British engineers use heat from an incinerator to power an electricity generator.

1879 Thomas Edison develops the electric lightbulb.

1882 Edison's Pearl Street Station, the first commercial power station, begins operation. It provides electricity to customers in a one-square-mile area in lower Manhattan.

1885 The first incinerator in the U.S. is built on Governor's Island in New York.

1932 The compactor garbage truck is developed.

1934 The U.S. federal government bans the practice of dumping trash into the ocean.

1937 Jean Vincenz designs the first sanitary landfill in Fresno, California.

1945 Destructors (municipal trash incinerators) fall into disuse.

1948 On Staten Island, Fresh Kills landfill opens to collect the trash of New York City.

1970 The first Earth Day is held on April 22.

1987 A Long Island garbage barge, the *Mobro*, is turned away by six states and travels 5,000 miles searching for a place to unload its cargo. The garbage is finally incinerated in Brooklyn, New York.

1993 BMW begins using methane gas from a landfill to power one of its manufacturing plants.

2002 Ireland imposes a tax on plastic grocery bags, which within weeks reduces their use by 94 percent.

2004 EPA declares Love Canal clean enough to take off the Superfund list. Toxins seeped into the Niagra Falls–area neighborhood in the 1970s when a landfill for chemicals under the ground leaked.

2006 Curbside recycling is widespread across the United States, with 8,660 programs nationwide.

2007 By this date, the EPA's Landfill Methane Outreach Program has helped develop 360 landfill gas programs, and has identified over 1,300 landfills to add to the list.

2009 As part of the economic stimulus package, President Barack Obama and Congress provide billions of dollars to encourage development of alternative energy, including waste-to-energy technologies.

Further Reading

Amsel, Sheri. *365 Ways to Live Green for Kids.* Avon, Massachusetts: F+W Media, 2009.

Fridell, Ron. *Earth-Friendly Energy.* Minneapolis: Lerner Publications, 2009.

Harlow, Rosie. *Garbage and Recycling.* Boston: Kingfisher Publications, 2002.

McMullan, Kate and Jim. *I Stink!* New York: HarperCollins, 2006.

Walker, Niki. *Biomass: Fueling Change.* New York: Crabtree Publishing Company, 2007.

Wilcox, Charlotte. *Earth-Friendly Waste Management.* Minneapolis: Lerner Publications Company, 2009.

On the Internet

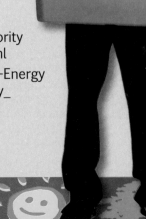

Delaware Solid Waste Authority Kids' Page
http://www.dswa.com/kids_club/index.htm

Earth Day website
http://www.earthday.gov/kids.htm

EIA Kids' Page: Waste to Landfills
http://www.eia.doe.gov/kids/energyfacts/saving/recycling/solidwaste/landfiller.html

EPA Student Center: Waste & Recycling
http://www.epa.gov/region5/students/waste.htm

The Rotten Truth About Garbage
http://www.astc.org/exhibitions/rotten/rthome.htm

Southeastern Chester County Refuse Authority
http://www.seccra.org/SECCRA_Power.html

Virtual Field Trip to a Baltimore Waste-to-Energy Plant http://www.eia.doe.gov/kids/energy_fungames/energyant_trips/trip_resco.html

Works Consulted

Barbalace, Kenneth. "The History of Waste." *EnvironmentalChemistry.com*. August 2003. http://EnvironmentalChemistry.com/yogi/environmental/wastehistory.html

Berger, John J. *Charging Ahead: The Business of Renewable Energy and What It Means for America.* New York: Henry Holt & Company, 1997.

California Energy Commission. "Waste-to-Energy and Biomass in California." http://www.energy.ca.gov/biomass/msw.html

DeCesaro, Jennifer, and Matthew H. Brown. *Bioenergy: Power, Fuels and Products.* Washington, D.C.: National Conference of State Legislatures, 2006.

Eddings, Amy. "Waste-to-Energy: Time to Reconsider?" WNYC, broadcast, November 28, 2005. http://www.wnyc.org/news/articles/54440

Energy Alternatives. Ed. Barbara Passero. Detroit, MI: Greenhaven Press, 2006.

Garbage and Recycling. Ed. Mitchell Young. Detroit, MI: Greenhaven Press, 2007.

Greenpeace. http://www.greenpeace.org.

Pahl, Greg. *The Citizen-Powered Energy Handbook: Community Solutions to a Global Crisis.* White River Junction, VT: Chelsea Green Publishing, 2007.

Rosenthal, Elizabeth. "Motivated by a Tax, Irish Spurn Plastic Bags." *The New York Times.* February 2, 2008.

Royte, Elizabeth. *Garbage Land: On the Trail of Secret Trash.* New York: Little, Brown & Company, 2005.

Waste Online. "History of Waste and Recycling." http://www.wasteonline.org.uk/resources/InformationSheets/HistoryofWaste.htm

Waste-to-Energy Research and Technology Council. http://www.seas.columbia.edu/earth/wtert/

Wood, John H., Gary R. Long, and David F. Morehouse. "Long Term World Oil Supply Scenarios." August 18, 2004. http://www.eia.doe.gov/pub/oil_gas/petroleum/feature_articles/2004/worldoilsupply/oilsupply04.html

U.S. Environmental Protection Agency Clean Energy. "Municipal Waste." http://www.epa.gov/solar/energy-and-you/affect/municipal-sw.html

U.S. Environmental Protection Agency Landfill Methane Outreach Program. http://www.epa.gov/lmop

Glossary

active face—A site of activity.

alternative energy—Energy obtained from sources other than fossil fuels, and that do not harm the environment.

bioreactor (BY-oh-ree-ak-tor)—A new type of landfill to which liquids, air, and bacteria are added to make the trash break down faster.

carbon dioxide—A naturally occurring gas in the atmosphere, produced by earth processes, animals, and burning fossil fuels.

carbon footprint—A measure of how much carbon dioxide results from an activity.

dehydrated (dee-HY-dray-ted)—With water removed.

district heating—A system for distributing heat and cool air to surrounding buildings, usually using steam.

fossil fuel—Energy sources drilled or mined from the earth, such as petroleum, oil, and coal.

global warming—An increase in the world's temperatures caused by the greenhouse effect.

incinerator (in-SIN-er-ay-tor)—A furnace that burns trash at high temperatures.

leachate (LEE-chayt)—Liquid that seeps out of a trash pile.

methane (MEH-thayn)—A naturally occurring gas in the atmosphere, produced in part by animals and by the chemical breakdown of trash in landfills.

natural gas—A gas formed in the earth over millions of years that can be burned as fuel.

post-consumer content—The amount of recycled material, previously used by someone, used to make a new product.

power grid—A system that distributes electricity throughout a region.

renewable (ree-NOO-uh-bul)—Able to be made again.

scrubbers—Chemicals, filters, or machines that clean dirty air inside a factory smokestack.

Superfund site—A site polluted by toxic wastes, where the U.S. Environmental Protection Agency has taken responsibility for its cleanup.

waste-to-energy—A process that uses trash to fuel an electricity generator.

Index

A versatile author, Claire O'Neal has published several books with Mitchell Lane, including *How to Use Wind Power to Light and Heat Your Home* from this series. She holds degrees in English and Biology from Indiana University, and a Ph.D. in Chemistry from the University of Washington. After five years of living in Seattle, she gained a deep respect for greener living. Claire composts, recycles, and tries to turn out the lights when she leaves the room. She lives in Delaware with her husband, two young sons, and a fat black cat.